The Battle of Bamber Bridge

The True Story

Derek Rogerson

Edited by Viv Ainslie

Published by Purple Parrot Publishing
Printed in the United Kingdom
First Printing, 2022
ISBN: Print: 978-1-8382769-2-8

Purple Parrot Publishing
www.purpleparrotpublishing.co.uk

Acknowledgements

Many of the events leading up to the actual battle are either first-hand accounts or accounts handed down through family involvement. In particular, I must thank Valerie Fell, who was the granddaughter of George Harrison - the landlord of the Hob Inn in 1943, for her invaluable contributions. My thanks also go to Michael Turner, Anne Baldwin, Jackie Kinnear, Nellie Shorrock, Linda Trafford, Brenda Lang, Julie Powell, Rolinda Bibby, Eunice Byers and many other Bamber Bridge residents for their photos and accounts of that fateful night in June 1943.

The account of the battle itself is mainly taken from personal or handed down experiences of many local residents, transcripts of the actual military trials that took place later that year, and newspaper accounts from the time relating to the battle.

Although the action scenes are true accounts of the actual battle, some of the soldiers' backgrounds and events and incidents prior to June 24th and much of the dialogue spoken during this period, particularly by the principle characters, may not be totally accurate. However, dramatic licence allows me to surmise that under the circumstances of the events portrayed, the pre battle incidents and conversations that occurred up to june 24th, are quite possibly in line with what could have happened and been said at the time.

Although we can never know the actual conversations that took place before and during the battle, dramatic licence allows us a degree of speculation. This being the case, much of the dialogue has been presumed but could have been uttered under the circumstances of the particular event being described.

Contents

Prologue

Fists, stones, and bullets flew in Bamber Bridge that fateful night in June 1943. As dawn broke and residents peered cautiously through curtained windows, they saw that the streets now ran red with the blood of the dead and wounded – and were afraid. But how did it all begin in this sleepy Lancashire town? The following pages will describe to you the true story of the battle and of some of the people involved in this infamous event.

Chapter 1

William Crossland

'Hey Billy, the mailman is coming up the track,' called out his father from the barn. 'Now who in blue blazes would be sending us mail I'd like to know? Go meet him Billy before the dogs see him off.'

William Crossland, better known as Billy to all who knew him, lived with his family on their little 10-acre smallholding, tucked away in a rural corner of Pittsylvania County in the state of Virginia.

It was early 1942 and the country had been at war since December 1941. Not that this had affected the good people of sleepy Pittsylvania much, apart from listening to the daily radio reports. Billy, with the rest of his family, had listened dutifully to the reports, with all but Billy showing any real enthusiasm to the unfolding events...

Billy was more than a little surprised to find that the large buff-coloured envelope that the mailman handed over to him was addressed to him. In all his 20 years on the farm he had never before received a letter, and after scrutinizing it from every possible angle, it was with shaking hands that he eventually opened it.

'What's it say son?' enquired his dad who was now standing by Billy's side with burning curiosity etched all over his black wrinkled face.

'It's from the draft board Pop, saying I gotta report to Fort Belvoir next Monday to start my basic training – Gee Dad, I've been conscripted into the army to fight for my country.' Noah, his aged dad, reflected on his son's announcement with mixed feelings. Sure, it was only right that the young black man should want to fight to keep his country free. But what did freedom really mean for Noah Crossland and his extended family. He and his forefathers had lived for many generations in this part of Virginia, but it had only been in the past 80 years or so that they had been released from slavery in the cotton plantations and officially classed as 'free American citizens.'

However, 'Jim Crow' laws were zealously observed in this part of the States and freedom for Noah and his family meant that because of their colour, among many other restrictions, they could not join the local golf club. Neither would they be allowed into the local cinema, apart from through the back door and into their own little area at the back of the auditorium. Yes, they could use the local bus service as long as they gave up their seat if a white person was standing.

This restricted lifestyle then had been the lot for the Crossland family. They and their black friends and neighbours had grown up with this inhuman and archaic system, and although there was some restrained resentment to their lot, particularly among the younger members of the family, they reckoned they were better off than most of their neighbours. This was probably due to Billy's extraordinary mechanical skills in not only keeping the family's ancient tractor running well past its sell-by date but doing the same for most of the close-knit community, including many of the white farmers. Not only did this give them some extra standing in the community, but it was said that Noah distilled the finest moonshine in the whole of Pittsylvania, much to the delight of his neighbours, both black and white.

Chapter 2

Lynn Adams

'Hey black boy! Watcha doing in here?' Are you old enough to be drinking beer?' questioned the overweight redneck guy seated on the adjacent stool in Murphy's Bar.

'What's it to you, fatso?' responded the young negro youth angrily. Lynn Adams had just finished a long and tiring shift at Kelly's Auto and had called into Murphy's for a quick drink before making his way home.

'Don't you black boys ever learn to speak civil to decent folk?' replied the redneck threateningly. 'Why for two pins I'd take you outside and knock some good manners into you,' he added mockingly. 'But I suppose that would be as useless as teaching my prize pig to wear a napkin when he's at the trough.' This last remark drew a few laughs from some of the other drinkers at the bar. Louie however was not laughing. All that day he'd been getting grief from his boss at the garage and this final insult was just one too many. The redneck never saw that huge black fist as it landed with a sickening thud on his jaw, knocking him clean off the bar stool. The bartender, a huge guy with arms like tree trunks, grabbed at Louie in a frantic attempt to restrain him. It was a bad move, as he then received similar treatment to the redneck who was now out cold.

Now it's not certain how this fracas would have developed if it had not been for the intervention of a recruitment sergeant and his buddy, who had also been enjoying what should have been a quiet drink at Murphy's. It did however take all their combined strength and army training to finally subdue the wild young negro.

'Now look here kid,' said First-Class Sergeant Franklin to the still enraged Louie. 'Reckon you could be in real trouble when the guy you hit comes round. Reckon you got two choices to make in the next five minutes. Stay here and face the consequences of those itchy fists or come with us down to the recruitment centre and sign some papers. Reckon Uncle Sam could do with a fighting boy like you in his army.' Louie was an impetuous young man of 21 but he was no fool. His short temper had got him into trouble on a number of occasions and he reckoned that this latest incident would probably see him behind bars. He was loathe to be involved with what he saw as a white mans' war but was wise enough to realise that it sure beat the alternative.

'Where do I sign?' he enquired; now resigned to his inevitable fate.

Chapter 3

Eugene Nunn

'Late again Nunn ,' cried Amos Walker jovially, the leader of the Ballard County Gospel singers. 'By the look of those oily hands, I reckon you been under that old Tin Lizzie of yours again. Reckon it's time you took it to the scrapyard and got yourself some more reliable wheels.' Eugene Nunn, better known as Gene to all who knew him, gave Amos and his fellow gospellers an apologetic grin before responding.

'You got me dead to rights there Brother Amos. Still, I reckon there's a few hundred miles left in old Lizzie yet if I treat her right,' his grin widening even further at the witty remark.

'Reckon we'll start without you next time,' Amos responded with a resigned shake of his head, knowing that this would probably never happen. Gene's extraordinary tenor voice was the mainstay of the choir. This coupled with his ability to fix anything mechanical was well known throughout the county. It made him almost as indispensable as his childhood sweetheart Sarah who played the organ and sang like an angel,

Eugene was the last of the younger male vocalists in the gospel singers' group. Not surprisingly all his young fellow balladeers had long since decided to take up arms to fight for their country. Gene had always considered himself a devout Christian and confirmed pacifist, and that the killing of his fellow men could never be justified in the eyes of the Lord.

However, these noble sentiments had recently taken quite a battering when the family had received that dreaded, black-edged telegram, informing them that their son and brother, who had been among the first to volunteer to serve his country as a medic, had been killed at the Battle of Bataan. Gene's long-held anti-war beliefs evaporated at the news. Tonight, would be the last time that his sweet tenor voice would be heard in that little church hall. He had signed the necessary forms and by this time tomorrow he would be well on his way to start his basic training at Fort Belvoir. Sarah had shed a few tears when she had heard the news but was proud of her Gene and the bold decision he had made.

Chapter 4

Roy Windsor and Ralph Ridgeway

Roy Windsor and Ralph Ridgeway were born and raised in the Southern States of the USA, and though slavery had been abolished many years before, negroes were still looked on and treated as second class citizens. What were known as the 'Jim Crow' laws were the order of the day in the Southern States, and segregation was practised in all walks of everyday life, including both work and play.

It was therefore not surprising to learn that the two white guys mentioned above, who knew no other way of life, other than that practised by their families and peers, treated members of the black community as an inferior race, who had to be kept in their place by words – or if necessary – actions.

When war broke out in 1941, both Windsor and Ridgeway demonstrated their patriotism to their country by enlisting at the first opportunity. Both were big strong young men and unsurprisingly were drafted into the Military

Police Force. This proved to be an appointment that suited them both, especially when after their initial training they were posted overseas to the UK.

They were more than happy when the posting was to the little Lancashire town of Bamber Bridge, to a camp where the majority of the soldiers were black. What a golden opportunity to establish their authority over their perceived inferiors. It did not take long for them to assert their 'Jim Crow' attitudes towards the black soldiers, which soon earned them the dubious distinction of being the most despised and hated men in the whole of Bamber Bridge.

Fort Belvoir

Chapter 5

Fort Belvoir

Army life proved to be tough at Fort Belvoir, although it was not the basic training that was causing grief for the black intake. If they thought that soldiering would bring universal camaraderie where all men were equal, then they were in for a harsh wake-up call. Far from leaving 'Jim Crow' to reap his misery in the civilian world, the military version was proving to be just as harsh, with segregation rife in all daily activities. There were separate canteens, blood banks, hospitals or wards, medical staff, barracks and recreational facilities for the black soldiers and white soldiers, and local white residents routinely slurred and harassed them.

There was initial disappointment at this turn of events, but, as in their civilian life, they had little choice but to grudgingly accept their lot.

Each evening, often after a hard day's training, found them making the best of their recreational time. Skills, honed as civilians, were often put to good use. The battered old piano in the canteen had been a magnet for Private William Crossland, and he soon proved to his comrades that he could sure 'tickle those ivories'. Those happy days around the piano in the parlour of the little farmhouse in Pittsylvania, where William had entertained his family, were once again created in the camp canteen. It was not long before his playing and singing in a high falsetto voice led to some of the other boys joining in with many of the popular ballads of the day. None more so than Private Eugene Nunn, whose gospel trained voice complemented well that of the talented piano player. Much to everyone's surprise, big Lynn Adams, who spent most of his free time in the gym or the boxing ring, amazed them all when, with his rich baritone voice, he joined in as William played the opening bars of the evergreen favourite, 'Smoke gets in your eyes'.

From that moment, an alliance was formed between the three of them. An alliance that would see them through some happy times in the service of their country, but as fate would eventually decree, it would unfortunately end in a tragedy that would affect them all.

In 1942, although black men were allowed to serve in the US armed services, they were not permitted to bear arms or join combat units. The military chain of command didn't think African Americans were fit for combat or leadership positions. They were mostly relegated to labour and service units, worked as cooks and mechanics, building roads, digging ditches and other such menial duties. Loading and unloading supplies from trucks and airplanes were common tasks for black soldiers, and for the few who did make officer rank, they could only lead other black men.

It was no surprise then, when basic training had been

completed, that the black soldiers stationed at Fort Belvoir were given their postings. Many went into pioneering or cookhouse units. Others, due to their civilian occupations, were drafted accordingly. This meant that those with mechanical skills, particularly with road vehicles, found themselves posted to the 1511th Quartermaster Truck regiment, which at that time was stationed in England, in a little provincial town in Lancashire, known as Bamber Bridge or as the locals called it – Brig.

As luck would have it, the three amigos, as William, Eugene and Lynn became known, were among the dozen or so who were to be posted to this regiment. It was just a few days later that news came through of their departure date from the United States to England – and there was great excitement among the ranks!

Raw recruits being put through their paces

Chapter 6

Off to pastures new

'Hey guys! Wait for me!' The kitbag thrown into the back of the military lorry was quickly followed by the huge frame of Lynn Adams as he vaulted nimbly into the midst of his fellow recruits. The two dozen or so black soldiers that made up the contingent had finished their basic training and had now been assigned to their military postings. This particular intake had all revealed their mechanical skills, and as such had been assigned to motor pools. They were now heading for the airport, from where they would be flying to Europe, where their particular skills would no doubt be put to good use in the 1511th Quartermaster Truck regiment.

'Anyone know where this godforsaken hole of Bumber Bridge is situated?' asked Louie as he dusted himself off.

'Think you'll find that the village is called Bamber Bridge buddy, and I believe there are a few attractions even in this little backwater,' replied Eugene, slipping another wad of gum into his mouth.

'Such as what,' Lynn demanded.

'Well, there are quite a few bars or pubs as they call 'em over there,' chimed in William Crossland. 'Although I believe the beer is served warm in England,' he added with a grin.

'Well let's hope the broads are hot then to make up for it,' Lynn responded to the amusement of his fellow troopers.

'Not that we'll be allowed anywhere near either of them I suppose' said William with an exaggerated sigh.

'Well, it won't be for the lack of trying,' replied Lynn. The further outburst of laughter from the recruits was so raucous that the driver thought he was carrying a pack of demented hyenas.

The short march from the railway station to Adams Hall Camp

Chapter 7

Arrival at Bamber Bridge

The flight from the US had been uneventful. The plane had touched down at Warton Airfield at noon in typical northern weather – it was pouring down. Feeling as downcast as the weather, the boys boarded the trucks that had been sent for them and were soon passing through the 13 miles or so of Lancashire countryside to their camp in Bamber Bridge.

On arrival in the small mill town, they were somewhat surprised when the trucks in which they were travelling stopped at the town's railway station. The small black contingent was met by Lieutenant Edwin Jones, who turned out to be the only black officer at the Adams Hall Camp. His first action was to take them into the station waiting room, where he proceeded to give them a brief lecture on how they were expected to behave as soldiers and guests in a foreign country.

The sun had managed to break through the clouds as the two dozen or so black soldiers marched in time from

Soldiers marching to camp

the station to their camp. On the way, their apprehensions as to how their presence would be received by the local community were bolstered by the smiles and clapping of the few people who lined the main Station Road that led to Mounsey Road, where the Adams Hall camp was situated. The cheering and flag-waving were punctuated by cries from a handful of young boys of what was destined to be a phrase heard many times on the streets of Bamber Bridge over the next couple of years or so – 'Any gum chum!'

Chapter 8

Adams Hall Camp

The mood of the newly arrived black contingent had been lifted by the greeting they had received as they marched in good order through the streets and into the camp. Adams Hall was principally a base for black American soldiers, apart from a few white officers that is, the acting commander of the camp, Major George C. Heris, and of course the Military Policemen or as they were better known, the MPs, whose barracks was not far from the main camp.

The camp was laid out in typical military fashion but had a good feel about it. As they marched to their billets, they quickly realised that here they would be free of the 'Jim Crow' segregation rules. There was not a building in the camp that was off limits. They were free to visit canteens, medical facilities and recreational halls without the fear of seeing the dreaded sign 'Whites Only'.

This new-found freedom was even further enhanced, when, after a good night's sleep and a hearty breakfast, they were summoned to the drill hall for a further briefing from black officer, Lieutenant Jones. From a raised platform, he informed them that in England there were no segregation laws, and when they were allowed out of the camp, they were free to go anywhere in the town, including all the public houses. He also reminded them that they were guests in the country, and to be on good behaviour at all times.

The thrill on hearing this news was dampened somewhat when the Lieutenant introduced MP Corporal Roy Windsor to give further guidance on what was expected of them outside the confines of the camp.

'Now listen well boys; you've heard the smooth version, now hear what it really means. These Limey's are a soft touch; they believe all men are created equal and should be treated as such. Fortunately, we know that this is not strictly true, and in God's own country we separate black from white. However, the good people of England have not yet experienced the dubious pleasure of living side by side with the negro, and me and my buddies are here to make absolutely sure that you don't step out of line. If you attempt any of your n****r tricks here, we will boot your black asses all the way to the guardhouse, and all privileges will be withdrawn for the duration! GOT IT?' thundered Corporal Windsor , with a stare that would have put the fear of God in the hardest of men.

'We OK to chew gum and fart without upsetting the natives then?' enquired Private Lynn Adams with a grin that brought a few stifled titters from his black comrades.

'See, it's smart-ass comments like that which do you black boys no favours. I've got my eye on you Adams, so I'd watch my step if I were you.' With that the MP stood down from the platform, allowing Lieutenant Jones to hand out the first evening passes that would permit the boys to venture unaccompanied onto the streets of Bamber Bridge.

Chapter 9

The Streets of Bamber Bridge

Privates Nunn, Adcroft and Crossland had become firm buddies due to their shared interests, and with a couple of their comrades, Privates Ogletree, and Wise, they took up their passes and ventured into the nearby town centre. Nearly every resident they passed, both young and old, gave them a warm and welcoming smile, which was unlike anything that they had ever encountered in their own country from white folk.

The little group decided to walk the full length of the town in the evening sunshine in order to get their bearings. They were surprised at the number and variety of shops along the main thoroughfare. It was the A6, better known as Station Road in its passage through the centre of the town, and part of a trunk road that ran from Luton to Carlisle.

What surprised them even more was the number of public houses they passed on their first foray into the town.

By the time they had reached The Olde Hob Inn, they made a unanimous decision to walk no further. Here before them lay what they imagined to be the quintessence of an old English pub, from its solid oak beams to the thatched roof; a sight that none of them had ever seen before.

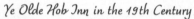

Ye Olde Hob Inn in the 19th Century

However, old habits die hard, yet their search for the door signed 'Blacks only' proved to be fruitless. And so they entered by the oak-studded front door, ducking their heads as they passed under the low stone lintel, bearing a polished wooden plaque informing all who entered the pub, in bold gold lettering, that a certain George Harrison was the licensee.

'Five beers please ma'am if that's OK,' Private Nunn asked of the young lady behind the bar.

'No problem boys,' she replied with a smile. 'Now will that be pints or halves, and by the way it's Doris not ma'am; I'm not royalty yet. I'm still waiting for my Prince Charming to come along,' she added with a twinkle in her eye. 'And I suggest you start with halves. Our beer takes a bit of getting used to after that gassy stuff they serve in America.' The five comrades joined in with the laughter that ensued.

'Well Doris, I reckon we'll take your advice, so halves it is then,' Private Adams replied. 'And don't you kid us. We can all see you're definitely queen of this castle.' The laughter that followed was joined in by the few locals in the pub at that time.

After an agreeable hour or so exchanging pleasantries with Doris and the other drinkers and being introduced to the mysteries of darts and dominoes, they left the Hob Inn to continue their tour. They all agreed that the welcome had been great, the fellow drinkers friendly, and the beer was in fact quite tasty, and not half as warm as they had been expecting.

Ye Olde Hob Inn in the 1970s

Chapter 10

Shall We Dance and the Double Clutchers

The new intake of troops soon settled into the routine of military life. The three amigos were particularly pleased with their lot, as in civilian life they were never happier than when messing about with engines and gearboxes. Their duties in the motor pool of the 1511th Quartermaster Truck regiment gave them every opportunity to do just that, and life was good.

It was not all work, however, and generally, the weekends were free unless an emergency occurred. On the Friday of their first week in the camp, Staff Sergeant William Byrd asked the boys if they were going to the dance that was held every Saturday night in the Recreation Hall. The boys exchanged puzzled looks as dancing usually required the attendance of members of the opposite sex. As they had already been warned about fraternizing with the local girls, they couldn't understand how dancing, as they knew it, could ever happen.

'Are you asking me to dance sarge?' asked Private Lynn Adams. 'Well, I'm flattered but you're not really my type,' he grinned.

'I'd rather stick pins in my eyes than dance with you, you big jerk,' laughed Sergeant Byrd. 'It's the fun-loving gals from Preston and Blackburn who provide us with partners. Every Saturday evening you can't move around the railway station for the broads arriving on what we call the 'Love Trains', and all heading to either the local pubs or the camp Recreation Hall, which serves very well as a dance hall. We do get a few of the local girls coming in but mostly it's the ones from the surrounding towns who come looking for a good time – if you know what I mean,' added the sarge, tapping his nose knowingly.

The highlight of the week for the three amigos usually took place after church parade on Sunday mornings. In the middle of the camp was a small field that the soldiers had turned into a baseball diamond. True, it was not quite the regulation size for a diamond, but they made good use of the space available The area was also used as a football pitch, but not the kind of the game that the Bamber Bridge residents were used to watching at either nearby Deepdale, the home of soccer club, Preston North End, or Ewood Park, where Blackburn Rovers played their matches. No, this was the rough, tough American version. A bit like English rugby with similar blood and aggression. The only time that the camp medical staff were really busy was after one of the football training sessions. Heaven only knows what the situation would have been like if they had ever played a competitive match.

But things were different with the baseball aficionados. They actually formed a team which, because of their connection to motorized transport, was known as the 'Double Clutchers'. Although the diamond was a bit primitive, it did allow the guys to play competitive matches

'Double Clutchers' practice for their big match

against similar makeshift teams of their compatriots, from nearby US camps at Washington Hall near Chorley and Warton in the Fylde area.

Although Babe Ruth and the like had nothing to fear from the three amigos, they made up for their lack of pure baseball skills with their enthusiasm. Private Nunn could pitch a mean curve ball, and big Private Adams, so rumour has it, had once hit a ball that had landed in the middle of Station Road. Whenever matches were staged at the camp, the Double Clutchers were cheered on by crowds of local townspeople, although it is believed that many of them who attended, such as local lad, 9-year-old Michael Turner, were only there for the 'goodies' handed out between innings.

The team really came to the notice of a wider audience when they played a charity match with local rivals, Washington Hall, at Deepdale. Apparently, the game was well attended from a novelty point of view. However, baseball never really captured the hearts of Lancashire folk, who considered it be nothing more than a 'grown up' version of rounders.

Chapter 11

Party Time

There was no doubt that the black American soldiers had endeared themselves to the locals. This was most apparent among the younger members of the town.

In a time when sweets were on ration, it mattered little among the children of Bamber Bridge as there always appeared to be a ready supply of Hershey Bars for those brazen enough to ask. Looking back, Brenda Scowcroft who was a young child at the time and Nellie Sherlock and Linda Trafford who were teenagers, remember this all too well. They recall that it was a rarity not to see a child with chocolate on their fingers or chewing on a wad of Wrigley's army ration gum.

However, what really cemented this endearing relationship was when the kids were treated to film shows. When the silver screen flickered into life, that Recreational Hall come cinema and theatre really rocked, as the young audience cheered the cowboy skills of Hopalong Cassidy

Anne Baldwin, sucking her thumb.

Joan and Rita Cuthbertson enjoying party time

and Roy Rogers or laughed long and loudly at the antics of 'The Three Stooges' and the ever-popular 'Laurel & Hardy'.

But according to sisters Joan and Rita Cuthbertson, the real vote winner was the numerous parties held in the Hall. The Christmas one was of course the highlight of the year, but it needed the flimsiest of reasons for the soldiers to set out the trestle tables, load them with goodies, and invite the children to come along and enjoy the feast. It really was a feast for the kids, as much of the party food on display from the military food store was not readily available in the local shops, due of course to wartime rationing.

The feasting was nearly always followed by a rousing singsong, and current favourites of the time such as 'Run Rabbit Run' and the 'Teddy Bears' Picnic' were belted out by the youngsters, often accompanied by Private William Crossland on the piano and Private Eugene Nunn with his trusty mouth organ.

Chapter 12

Work, Play and Gifts

Fraternising with the local ladies was not allowed, although it was difficult, if not impossible to enforce. The reasons for this were twofold.

Firstly, the camp employed a fair number of local people, most of them women whose duties were mainly domestic and ranged from cleaning to cooking.

However, there was also a very special group of local ladies based at the camp. They were employed by the American Red Cross and carried out a range of duties from nursing to a variety of domestic roles, including working in the camp's Aero Club Canteen.

One of these ladies was Lillian Johns, who, through her niece, Brenda Lang, has told of the many memorable moments that she and her fellow workers enjoyed at the Adams Hall camp. It was inevitable that friendships were formed with the black soldiers, mostly platonic but romances were not unheard of.

The second reason was far more commercially based, particularly among the younger women of the town. Ever since the outbreak of war, the simple delights of dressing up and applying a bit of 'lippie' that were pleasures enjoyed pre-war, had all but disappeared. Cosmetics were expensive and hard to find. This was because everything, including the ingredients used to make them, were used mostly for war efforts. The little left over for civilian life was rationed. Because everything was scarce, women had to be creative and resourceful: if they wanted to dye their hair, they could only use vegetable dyes.

Nylon stockings were nothing more than a half-remembered dream. However, Bamber Bridge ladies were imaginative and not short of ideas when stockings were not available. First, they applied neat gravy browning to their legs, before getting a friend to draw a line down the back to represent the seam. Oh what joy it must have been to have a friend who could draw a straight line. This was all very well if the weather stayed dry, but woe betide the girl who got caught in the rain!

Now all this messing about became redundant for the girl who had an American soldier for a friend. Lipstick, powder, and paint appeared to be in ready supply at the camp's PX Store, and how on earth they managed to get hold of nylon stockings is anybody's guess – but they did, and how the local ladies looked kindly on the soldiers' enterprise. Not everybody appreciated the 'gifts that kept on coming'. The local lads were up against it as young Raymond Almond knew only too well. 'Stealing our women they are,' he was heard to say on many an occasion. Well not quite; but then again, a bag of chips from the local chippy on the first date was no match for a Max Factor lipstick, or a pair of 15 denier nylons.

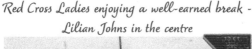

Red Cross Ladies enjoying a well-earned break - Lilian Johns in the centre

Chapter 13

Strained Relations

These were the happy times shared by the black soldiers and the local residents. Unfortunately, this convivial relationship was often put to the test by the presence of the all-white 234th US Military Police Unit, that was stationed at the North end of the town. It appeared that they had found it difficult to understand why the local population insisted on treating the black soldiers as their equals. By the same token, the majority of the locals found it equally disturbing why the MPs should treat the black soldiers as second-class human beings. It always appeared that the MPs used the slightest reason to come down on the soldiers; at best they tore into them for their very presence and at worst arrested them if they had the audacity to answer back.

The three amigos had decided to visit one of the other many public houses in the town. In their ignorance, they had not realized that this particular pub was one favoured by the MPs. Not that they were actually barred from entering the premises, but, in their ignorance, it appeared that they had broken some unwritten pact. As they approached the bar, they were followed in by a small group of locals. Private Eugene Nunn was about to place an order for beers when he was accosted by an MP who had been drinking with a companion.

'You can't serve those n*****s when there are white folk waiting to be served. Now stand back you three idiots and let the good white folks order their drinks.' There followed an uneasy silence until the landlord spoke up.

'A penny from a black man sits as well in my till as one from a white man,' he announced with authority and turning to the soldiers he asked, 'Now lads, what can I get you?'

The atmosphere in the pub turned decidedly frosty, although this was no fault of the group of young men who had followed the soldiers in and who were now laughing at the way the arrogant MP had apparently been put in his place. Corporal Roy Windsor, the MP who had issued the edict to the landlord, was fuming. He saw this as his authority being undermined - and by black man as well.

'Where are your passes?' he demanded of the three amigos.

'In our pockets,' Private Lynn Adams responded. 'Where's yours?'

'That's insubordination you black savage,' replied the now red-faced MP, bristling with rage. 'I've a good mind to arrest you for that foolish remark,' he added vehemently. At that moment, his drinking companion and fellow MP, Private First-Class Ralph Ridgeway, placed his hand on his shoulder and calmly whispered,

'Leave it this time Roy. There's no harm done, and just think of all that paperwork for a charge that may not stick with all these witnesses about.' Roy Windsor saw the sense in his companion's logic and turning to Lynn Adams informed him that this was his lucky night, but if he stepped out of line once more, then he wouldn't be so lucky next time. Inside however, he was incandescent with pent up fury, and he vowed that this incident would not go unpunished.

Chapter 14

The Colour Bar that Backfired

The events of that particular night gnawed painfully at Roy Windsor's misguided sense of fair play. As each day passed, he considered numerous ways of exacting his revenge on the black soldiers in general and the three amigos in particular. It was a casual remark by one of his fellow MPs that gave him what he considered to be the perfect solution. His colleague had said that such an occurrence would never happen in the States, as the negros were not even allowed to enter many of the countries' drinking establishments, particularly those in the Southern states.

That's it, he thought. Let's get a colour bar imposed in the pubs, so that the black soldiers are only allowed to drink within the confines of the camp. Recent racial events back home in Detroit had left many of the black soldiers uneasy, giving MP Windsor all the justification he needed to press home his suggestion. After obtaining the necessary permission from his commanding officer, he met with Major George C. Heris, the acting commander of Adams Hall Camp. Although at first reluctant, after hearing MP Windsor's exaggerated reports of incidents that had supposedly occurred in the town's pubs, he eventually agreed to meet with the landlords and licensees of all the public houses, in the Camp recreational hall, where he urged them, for the sake of safety and security, to impose a colour bar at the earliest opportunity.

The landlords and licensees agreed to discuss the proposal made by the Major and return the following day with their answer…

It was reported that the licensees held a meeting, which probably proceeded along the following lines.

'What's your thoughts about this 'ere colour bar lads?' asked one of the landlords of his peers.

'Well, it's not very British I must say,' replied one.

'I agree with you,' responded another. 'And why should these Yanks be telling us how to conduct our business,' he added. 'The only time there appears to be any trouble is when the MPs are about. There's certainly no love lost between them and the black lads, that's for sure,' he concluded. It was then that one of their number made the little speech, which convinced some of them that a colour bar of sorts was indeed a very good idea.

'Don't know about you lads, but 'ere in my pub, for every penny spent by the MPs, the black lads spend a shilling. Reckon we should commence that colour bar as soon as possible. Shall we let the Major know of our decision?'

Not all of the landlords were happy with this proposal, and many of them thought it best not to apply a colour bar but to let anyone, despite their colour or creed, and providing that they were of legal age and behaved themselves, to drink in their establishment. However, there were three brave souls that believed that a colour bar with a difference was a very good idea …

'Hey Roy, come and have a look at the notices that have gone up in three of the pubs,' said one of his MP colleagues. As he finished his breakfast, Roy's face lit up at this news.

'Yea, I've been expecting this,' he beamed. 'Is it about the colour bar?'

'I think you should come into town and see for yourself,' answered his colleague. If anger had been an explosive, then no doubt Corporal Roy Windsor would have been blown to smithereens. In three of the town's pub windows was the same handwritten notice –

It was obvious that such a ruling could never have been enforced, and yet the landlords of the three pubs had made their point. An uneasy peace ensued after the incident.

Unfortunately, it was not to last. The rift between the black soldiers and the MPs grew even wider. The town became a powder keg and sooner or later the fuse would be lit.

George Harrison -
Landlord of the Hob Inn

George's wife Edith, daughter Doris, grandson
Derek and granddaughter Valerie in mum's arms.

Chapter 15

Those Happy Times

Although the black soldiers were welcomed in most of the town's pubs, there was no doubting which one had become their favourite watering hole – Ye Olde Hob Inn. Whether it was the quaintness of the pub, the quality of the beer, or the welcome they received from the landlord George Harrison, his wife Edith and daughter Doris is anyone's guess. The pub was also frequented, not only by the local townspeople, but also by British military personnel of both sexes, and the atmosphere that pervaded was, on the whole, most convivial.

Edith had a particular empathy towards the black GIs. She had often been heard to remark that they were all somebody's sons or sweethearts, who were far from their homes and loved ones. They had come all the way from America to help us fight the war against the Germans and would always be made to feel welcome in the Hob Inn.

The cordial atmosphere that existed in this popular pub

Black Soldiers enjoy a drink outside the Hob Inn

was best seen whenever the piano player struck those first musical notes. This occurred on most evenings, much to the delight of all the patrons. Karaoke had not yet been introduced to the world but this didn't stop anybody who could hold a tune from standing up and giving it their best shot. It was quite surprising at the number of passable vocalists that frequented the Hob Inn. None more so than the landlord's son-in-law Joe, who entertained on many evenings, with his mother-in-law Edith joining in the singsong along with the rest of the patrons in the 'snug'. Landlord George often said that Joe's rendition of 'Red Sails in the Sunset' was good enough to be heard on the wireless – but then again, maybe he was a little bit biased.

It was however when the regular pianist rose to 'wet his whistle' that the real concert started. It was then that Private William Crossland took the opportunity to display his keyboard skills, and his playing of all the ragtime classics had the patrons enthralled, and their clapping and cheering were such that it was a wonder it didn't raise the thatch from the old pub's roof.

There were of course quieter moments, and you could

almost hear a pin drop when Privates Nunn and Adams joined their comrade in renditions of the old Stephen Foster songs, such as 'I Dream of Jeannie' and 'Beautiful Dreamer'.

George Harrison - Bandmaster

They never did forget where they were, and, much to the delight of the pub patrons, always closed their little musical contribution with a rousing version of 'She's a Lassie from Lancashire'.

Yes it was nights such as this that helped to cement the goodwill between people from two different nations – What a pity then that it was fated not to last.

Detroit Riots June 1943

Chapter 16

The Touchpaper

It was on a night such as this that the trouble first started. The mood in the camp had been subdued over the past few days, when news of the Detroit racial riots on June 20th had reached the ears of the black soldiers. The military authorities had tried to keep a lid on the story, fearing that it may cause further unrest among the black troops stationed in the UK. It proved to be an event impossible to keep quiet, having been widely reported on the radio and in the British press.

However, there was a birthday to celebrate on the night of June 24th, 1943, and despite the disturbing news from back home, where better for such a celebration than at the Hob Inn? The three amigos were no fools and were very much aware that they were probably at the top of MP Roy Windsor's hate list. As a consequence, they always made sure that, when they were out on the town, they were properly dressed in their Class A uniforms, and that their passes were always correct and up to date.

On that particular evening in June, Privates Adams and Crossland were dressed in their Sunday best uniforms and had ensured that their passes would satisfy the most officious of MPs, the said Corporal Windsor and his buddy in arms, Private Ridgeway in particular.

It was somewhat unfortunate that the third member of the trio, Private Eugene Nunn, was unable to join them that evening. He had been delegated to pick up a new truck from a US army camp in Manchester and attempts to escape this duty had been fruitless. There was a chance that if he put his foot down, he could probably make it back to Bamber Bridge for 'last orders'.

It was somewhat unfortunate for him that the handover did not go as smoothly as he had hoped, and it would be touch and go as to whether he would arrive back in Bamber Bridge before pub closing time. Being stopped by an MP patrol for a paper check just outside Preston did not help things, and the clock at St Saviour's church was just striking 10 when, with a screech of brakes, he pulled up outside the Hob Inn.

As the fates would decree on that particular night, the MPs on town patrol just happened to be Corporal Windsor and Private Ridgeway. They were parked up across the road from the pub and observed Private Nunn alighting from the cab of his truck.

'Best let him know that it's too late to buy a drink,' sighed Private Ridgeway as he attempted to leave the jeep in order to stop him. Roy Windsor grabbed his companion's arm and instructed him to let Nunn enter the pub.

'This could be the opportunity we've been waiting for to

nail those black bastards,' he informed young Ralph. 'Give it a couple of minutes and we'll follow him in,' he added with a wicked grin.

Now when things go wrong for certain people, the fates sometimes decide that they go wrong big time. As the two MPs entered the pub they observed Doris, the landlord's daughter handing Eugene Nunn a small bottle of beer. She was aware that it was past closing time but had felt sorry for Eugene after his long drive and had seen no harm in slipping him this one bottle and reminding him to be discreet.

Under normal circumstances, the event would have passed without further ado. Unfortunately, it was just the sort of incident that Roy Windsor had been waiting so many weeks for.

'Hey soldier; what do think you're doing?' he hollered. 'Purchasing alcohol after 10 pm is against the law and an arrestable offence. Now give the nice lady the bottle back and come quietly with us.'

'He wasn't buying it sir,' spoke up Doris bravely. It was a present from me.'

'You in the habit of buying presents for n*****s are you?' sneered the MP. 'I thought you would have had more sense.' At this derogatory remark, the atmosphere in the pub turned decidedly frosty. There were rumblings from all sides at what was perceived as a harsh racist and uncalled for reaction from the MPs. Roy Windsor realised he was in danger of losing the moral high ground but was in no mood to back down.

'What are you doing out in a field jacket Nunn ?' MP Windsor continued. 'I reckon that constitutes being improperly dressed. I'd better have a look at your pass as well, seeing as you don't seem able to conduct yourself properly as a soldier of the US army.' Private Nunn handed him his pass, which of course was to allow him to travel to Manchester and back.

'I thought as much, an incorrect pass. Reckon I'm gonna have to take you in after all.'

'Hey Windsor! You know exactly what the situation is here,' spoke out Private Lynn Adams, advancing towards the MPs with a bottle in his hand. 'Eugene is not with us. He's just returned from official military duty, and that's what his pass is for.'

'You questioning my authority Adams?' snapped the MP angrily, drawing his gun and pointing it at the unruly GI. 'I've a good mind to arrest you as well.' This unprecedented action was diffused somewhat by the intervention of black Staff Sergeant William Byrd, and the MP returned his gun to its holster. Unfortunately, the unrest among the black soldiers was increasing with every minute that passed. The two MPs sensed the growing hostility, and in an attempt to restore their authority, ordered all the black troops out of the pub.

The landlord, George Harrison, had been watching the escalating issue with some concern, determined not to intervene unless absolutely necessary. This latest command from the MPs proved to be the final straw that prompted his angry reaction.

'This is my pub, and I'll decide who stays and who goes, and I reckon it's you two who should make yourself scarce before you realise you have bitten off more than you can chew – now clear off!'

'Come on Roy, let's do as he says,' advised MP Ridgeway to his overwrought colleague. 'Let's return to the barracks and call up some of the guys. We can then return and show them that we are not to be messed with.'

As they made their way back to the jeep, Private Adams, fuelled by alcohol and sensing some sort of hollow victory over the bullying MPs, hurled the bottle he was holding at the jeep. It was a foolhardy action that made the departing MPs more determined than ever to exact swift retribution.

Chapter 17

The Match

As the little group of black soldiers made their way up Station Road to their camp in Mounsey Road, they were in high spirits. It appeared that they had got one over the MPs, and as one of their numbers remarked, 'Dey ran across dat road like whipped dogs with dere tails between dere legs.

Station Road

Dey nearly jumped out of dere lily-white skins when dat bottle hit the windscreen.'

The laughter that ensued was rudely interrupted by the roar of a jeep in which there were four MPs, all armed to the teeth as they sped up the road towards the surprised soldiers. Their official intention was to arrest who they considered to be the ringleaders of the trouble that had erupted in the Hob Inn. However, it was obvious that before this they wanted nothing more than to teach the unruly mob an unofficial lesson for daring to question their authority.

As the MPs jumped from their jeeps, it was no surprise to the black soldiers to see that the military policeman leading his fellow MPs was none other than Corporal Roy Windsor, closely followed by his ever-present sidekick, Private Ridgeway.

It was now that the pent-up rage of the black GIs exploded. Fuelled by the recent distressing news of the violence shown to their fellow African Americans in Detroit, they waded into the MPs with nothing more than their bare fists and stones that they picked up from the garden of a Mrs Dimmock, who lived on Station Road. It was soon clear to see by the small knot of spectators that had gathered, that they were getting the better of the exchanges.

Realising their situation, a few of the MPs drew their guns and waved them threateningly at the baying mob.

'Where's that n****r who threw a bottle at me?' screamed Corporal Windsor, brandishing his colt.

'Yea, I'm sorry about that,' came the response from Private Adams, who was in the thick of the action. 'I should have shoved it up your skinny white ass, but not to worry, I have another one here that should fit very nicely.' With that, he advanced menacingly towards his adversary. Two shots rang out from among the armed MPs, and one bullet struck Private Adams in the neck. It proved not to be fatal. The second bullet struck a Private Ogletree in the body. Fortunately, again it was not fatal but did end any further involvement in the skirmish from the wounded GIs.

This shooting appeared to temporarily diffuse the situation, and the little crowd that had gathered began to disperse. The MPs helped their injured colleagues into the jeeps, and sped off back to their barracks, leaving the black soldiers to help their own injured comrades back to the Adams Hall camp on Mounsey Road as best they could.

As well as a number of brave locals who observed the pitched battle from a safe distance, it had also been witnessed by a Mrs Baldwin and her daughter Vera from the window of their home at 294 Station Road. Little did they realise at the time that they were to act as prosecution witnesses at the trial of the black soldiers, which would be held later that year.

View of the riot site from the window of 294 Station Road

Chapter 18

Return to Camp

The black soldiers carried their half-conscious wounded comrades into the medical dispensary, where their wounds were cleaned and dressed. The camp medical officer informed Private Adams that he had been extremely lucky. Another couple of inches to the right and he would have arrived back at the camp, not as a casualty, but as a corpse.

The chief medical officer on duty, after careful examination, deemed that in both cases the wounds were serious enough for the men to be hospitalised, and they were sent by ambulance as stretcher cases to a US Station hospital in Warrington. As he was being carried out, Private Ogletree was in no mood to be pacified and shouted for all his fellow comrades to hear, 'I'm fighting and I'm still fighting. Are you not going to get those guys?'

Language of this nature, coming from one of the victims of a supposed unfair attack, would certainly serve to influence the sympathies of his fellow soldiers, and incite them to acts of violence and breaches of the peace. Ogletree, therefore, became one of the principal originators of the mutiny that followed.

In the recreation hall, the shaken little gang, after hearing Ogletree's fiery declaration, discussed the ugly happenings of the evening with the rest of their comrades. Feelings ran high when those who had not been present at the fracas learned of the shootings of Adams and Ogletree. The atmosphere among the black soldiers became more heated. They convinced themselves that this would not be the end of the matter and that the MPs would escalate the situation They now firmly believed that they would not be satisfied until they had killed at least some of their numbers.

News of the riot had by now reached the ears of the acting commanding officer, Major George Heris. He called all the men together, about 200 in number, and on the surface appeared to understand their frustrations. With the assistance of black officer Lieutenant Edwin Jones, he then promised that he would investigate the matter the following day, and see that justice was done – if only it had been that easy!

This appeared to appease a number of the black soldiers, who then retired to their quarters. Unfortunately, the majority of the men were not convinced by the Major's efforts of appeasement. Descriptions of the earlier disorder in town became distorted and somewhat exaggerated. The young soldiers, most of them in their early 20s, became excited, and a degree of hysteria swept through their ranks.

Even at this stage of proceedings, the high emotions exhibited by the soldiers could possibly have been cooled by the correct intervention from their officers. Unfortunately, there were a number of non-commissioned officers, who were responsible for indirectly inciting the soldiers. To make matters worse, there was almost a complete failure on the part of the more senior officers to assert authority over their men, and very little or any effort was made to prevent the disorder that inevitably ensued.

Irrational talk continued among the soldiers regarding the earlier shooting of their comrades, and they convinced themselves that more of them would become victims of the despised MPs.

No one can be sure who it was, but from the ranks of the assembled black soldiers, a strident voice called out, 'I ain't dying like no rat in a hole. Reckon it's time we got our retaliation in first. Who's with me for the guns?' The locks on the various gun store doors proved to be no deterrent for desperate men, and soon a large number of the GIs, who were assembled that night, had armed themselves with carbines or rifles, before marching down to the camp's main gates.

At the same time, a band of soldiers entered the motor pool, and a number of trucks were stolen and driven

Mounsey Road more recently

around the camp, with the occupants firing their guns indiscriminately. One truck was stopped by Major Heris, but another overtook it and crashed through the main gates and out onto Mounsey Road with the assembled soldiers cheering at this show of defiance to military authority.

Major Heris once more approached the men and gave direct and positive orders to junior and non-commissioned officers, to assemble the men and march them away from the gates. Unfortunately, the orders issued by the various officers were totally ignored by the men. Major Heris himself then gave orders in a loud voice to the assembled group, to form into lines and return to their respective company areas. But this order was also not obeyed by the men – and anarchy reigned throughout the camp.

Chapter 19

Overture to the Battle

It is possible that this open show of defiance could have petered out peacefully, especially when Lieutenant Edwin Jones, the only black officer in the camp, appeared to have instilled some measure of calm among the men. However, after the initial failure of Major Heris and his officers to restore order, the acting camp commander decided on a plan of action that had a direct and devastating bearing on what happened next.

At about 11 pm, Major Heris made a telephone call to the main Military Police detachment in Preston. As a result of this call, a large detachment of MPs left Preston and drove to Bamber Bridge. The detachment was commanded by Captain Herman Hech and consisted of 12 military policemen. The convoy was composed of an armoured scout car and two quarter-ton trucks. On the second of the trucks, a large machine gun had been mounted. The MP contingent arrived at the main gate of the Adams

Hall Camp and shone flashlights over the camp until such intimidating action was stopped by the commander of the detachment, Captain Hech.

He was then requested by Major Heris to take his men and vehicles out of sight of the camp and stand by for an emergency call if required. The MP detachment departed and drove south on Station Road, in the direction of the main part of Bamber Bridge.

News of the arrival of the military police with the armoured car and mounted machine-gun spread with rapidity throughout camp, and it was evident from what happened next that the purpose of the visit was magnified and distorted out of all proportion. There were shouts of 'The white MPs are here with machine guns. Let's get the rifles. They are at the gates with machine guns and are coming in tanks.' The anger, resultant from news of the shooting of Ogletree and Adams, had very much subsided, but following this latest visit of the military police, there was an obvious resurgence of tension and hysteria among the black soldiers. There then followed a display of mob psychology, which in turn prompted a fear approaching a near frenzy. Men ran through company streets and areas shouting and yelling. Rifle shots from within camp became more numerous during the next 10 minutes or so. The sound of motor vehicles being 'warmed up' and motors racing filled the air. Several vehicles were driven from the motor parks and into the main camp roads, and some of them were driven from the camp itself.

There had been relatively few men with rifles at that point. This all changed when the heavily armed MPs had made their appearance at the camp gate. Soon after the arrival of the MPs, even more armed black soldiers were to be seen in the camp – if only they had been sensible and stayed there!

Regrettably, sensible behaviour among the black soldiers was now in very short supply. The red mist had descended, clouding out any rational thoughts or judgement. They now believed that they were committed to taking the attack to their perceived enemies. The injustice of the day, coupled with years of subjugation and in light of the recent race riots in Detroit, predestined that they were now resolute to show that enough was enough. And how better than to vent their sense of injustice against a group of fellow Americans, who epitomised the whole white race, that had never shown them even an ounce of respect.

Chapter 20

The Battle

Black soldiers of an uncertain number, many armed with rifles and carbines, which had been secured without authority from the company supply rooms, and carrying ammunition taken from the regimental supply room and the guardhouse ammunition room, escaped from camp during darkness. Several were seen climbing over a fence at the rear of the camp. These men, together with those in the two-ton truck and other vehicles that left the camp, formed marauding parties wandering about Bamber Bridge for several hours committing various acts of violence.

In an effort to contain the riot to the immediate area of the camp, Major Heris ordered the local police to close the level crossing gates on the town's railway line; a track that neatly bisected Bamber Bridge into two distinct areas.

Word was hurriedly conveyed to the crossing keeper who quickly carried out the order and within minutes the gates clanged shut, blocking off the free passage to all vehicular traffic. However, the authorities had not factored in the determination of angry men who were hell-bent on doling out retribution for what they had perceived as a grave miscarriage of justice.

The stout wooden gates proved to be no barrier to a two-ton military vehicle driven at high speed, and with a thunderous crash they were torn asunder as if they had never been there. The mutineers now had the total run of the town in which to run amok.

Despite the lateness of the hour, there were still a few people on the streets of the town. Young Doreen Byers was making her way home to Mounsey Road when she was approached by two black soldiers. They told her to run home as quickly as possible as there was likely to be some shooting. It was then that they observed the callipers on her legs and realised that this would be difficult for the girl. With no more ado, they then picked her up and carried her quickly to the front door of her house; much to the relief of her anxious parents.

Another person nearly caught in the crossfire was Eunice Byers's father, Charles Byers. He was returning home to his little grocery shop on Station Road after a night out at his local club. He was fortunate though, as whilst there was plenty of shouting, the gunfire had not yet started.

Eunice Byers - now 104-years-old

Charles locked the front door and told the family members not to go out as there had been some trouble with the black soldiers at the Hob Inn. His daughter Eunice found this quite exciting, not realising yet how this 'trouble' would quickly escalate into a full-blown shooting match. Despite her father's concerns, Eunice pressed her face close to the window. It was then that she heard the noise of approaching vehicles, travelling at high speed. They turned out to be two army jeeps, full of military policemen; their faces grim and determined.

Charles thought his family would be safer upstairs, but it didn't stop Eunice from again looking out of the window, where she now had a bird's eye view of the action that was developing. She saw a group of black soldiers running up the road, and that's when the shooting started. She was somewhat startled when she saw, crouching in the shadows opposite the little shop, a black soldier holding something that appeared to be a gun. There then came the crack of yet another rifle being discharged, followed by the ominous sound of breaking glass. On hearing this Charles, ordered his daughter to come away from the window as it could easily have been the target for the next stray bullet.

All this activity had at first been quite exhilarating for Eunice, and although she had witnessed a few unusual incidents in her work at Police Headquarters at Hutton, nothing as exciting as what she was now witnessing had ever occurred in her hometown of Bamber Bridge. However, when told the following day of the carnage that had ensued, her previous feeling of excitement was replaced by one of deep sorrow.

The shooting could be heard all over the town, much to the distress of youngsters 12-year-old Tom Sharples, who at that time lived in School Street, and six-year-old Joan Gainer, who lived in the now long demolished Stone Row. Little did either of them realise at that troubling moment in their young lives, that just a few years later they would meet, fall in love, and eventually become man and wife. A heart-warming story that they have related to their grandson Danny Lyons on many occasions.

As the battle grew in intensity, one group composed of about 20 black soldiers, armed with rifles and carbines, reached a point in the southern part of Bamber Bridge, near the intersection of the Chorley and Wigan roads. They fired several shots near the home of a Mr Ashcroft, who foolishly went to the front door of his home to see what all the commotion was about. One of the soldiers warned him to get back inside as there was going to be a battle. Some of the armed men hid behind a stone wall, while two others crouched on the ground. These men then went in the direction of the Hob Inn, and soon after, much yelling and shooting was heard by Mr Ashcroft.

Sometime later, another group of about twelve armed soldiers, went over the wall surrounding Mr Ashcroft's home. From there, they then went down Station Road in the direction of Hob Inn. It was about 12:30 am when Mr Ashcroft heard more shooting, which continued for about an hour. Mr Ashcroft and his wife became extremely nervous and frightened on hearing the continuing shooting, Understandably, they kept well away from the doors and windows.

Another group of armed soldiers then approached the 'Queens Hotel', which is located on Church Road in the southern end of Bamber Bridge, not far from the Hob Inn. At about 11:15 pm on the 24th, Arthur Laidler, the proprietor of the Queens Hotel, heard shooting and upon going out to investigate the disturbance, he saw twenty or thirty black soldiers armed with rifles, running down Chorley Road in the direction of Bamber Bridge.

One soldier called out loudly to Mr Laidler, 'You better get inside boss. There's going to be plenty of shooting.' As he hurried indoors, another soldier shouted, 'Shoot the b****r.' Two of the soldiers discharged their rifles, but fortunately not directly at the landlord, and the shots passed safely over the roof of the hotel. Mr Laidler and his wife, although badly shaken, were not harmed.

Another group of six black soldiers were seen at about 11:15 pm on Station Road, at a point opposite the police station. They were all armed with either rifles or carbines. Two jeeps, filled with MPs, passed south on Station Road, coming from the direction of Preston, and they were fired on. Three more MP jeeps then passed heading south and they were also fired on. During this period, frequent rifle shots coming from

Bamber Bridge Police Station

Adams Hall Camp were heard by both Sergeant Lawrence Constable and Sergeant Ike Fell. They were County Police Officers stationed at Bamber Bridge and were on duty at the police station on that turbulent night. There was also a large number of local residents, who had come to the police station to seek protective shelter from the mayhem that was occurring on the streets of their once-peaceful town. Most of them chose to remain there until later that morning as it was far from safe to venture out into the public streets.

One man who did so was Edward Brindle. Despite the shooting, which was still continuing, he left the relative safety of the police station at about 2:40 am and proceeded south on Station Road towards his house. Before he reached the safety of his home, he encountered four black soldiers, all armed with rifles, sitting on a wall opposite the bank, situated on the corner of Mounsey Road. As he entered the door of' his house, a hail of bullets was fired in his general direction. Fortunately, he was not hit, but the bullets did make holes in the walls of the bank, which could be seen for many years after the battle and served as a chilling reminder of that infamous night and early morning in June 1943.

A little later, Major Heris ordered two of his officers to leave the camp and drive into the town in an effort to round-up the mutinous soldiers and return them to camp. After turning out of Mounsey Road, they drove south down Station Road. Near to the Queens Hotel public house, they encountered three black soldiers dressed in fatigues and all carrying rifles. The armed soldiers ordered the officers to halt, which they did. At this point, the soldiers began to shoot at the officers. One startled officer jumped out of the jeep and ran into an air-raid warden's house. The other officer took the wheel and backed the jeep around into a side street and sought refuge in a private home. Shots were heard a few minutes later, apparently aimed at the officers' vehicle. Neither officer was hurt in this nasty confrontation, but as they feared for their lives, they failed in their duty of taking any of the black soldiers back to camp.

One of the MPs, who was answering the call for assistance from Major Heris, left Preston at about 11 pm. He was driving a government half-ton Dodge truck. When he reached a point between Hopwood Street and Mounsey Road in Bamber Bridge, he heard a number of rifle shots. Something hit him in the face and the next day two pieces of brass were removed from the left side of his face. On further inspection, sixteen bullet holes were found in the front door of the truck. This MP had indeed been extremely lucky to escape with just superficial wounds, after yet another particularly ugly encounter.

The bullet ridden truck

Another of the camp's officers had been absent from the camp on official duties during that day. At about 11 pm, he was returning to the camp in a command car. As he was turning from Station Road into Mounsey Road, he heard a couple of rifles or carbines being discharged. About halfway down Mounsey Road, a truck stood crosswise across the street blocking his passage. The officer stopped and parked his car close to the truck. One of the black soldiers shouted, 'Cut the lights and switch the motor off.' He complied and waited about five minutes or so, and then attempted to drive around the truck. There then followed further shots aimed in the direction of his car. One shot went through the windscreen of his car but as luck would have it missed the officer. Further shots were aimed at the door of the car. This time he was not so lucky, and he received three bullets in his left leg and two in his right. When the shooting eventually ceased, he was ordered out of the car. A voice then instructed him to advance with his hands up. The unlucky officer, although severely wounded, struggled out of the car and was ordered to go to the rear of it. He was surprised to see the angry faces of between twenty or thirty armed black soldiers. On seeing his wounds, one of them called out, 'This is one of our officers.' When they saw the seriousness of his wounds, one of the black soldiers climbed into the driver's seat and took the wheel, while a second soldier assisted the injured officer into the vehicle. They then drove him to the camp's medical dispensary, where his wounds were cleaned and dressed. However, his wounds were considered serious and he was then taken to the US military hospital in Warrington.

It was around the area of Co-operative Street that the battle reached its climax. It was here that the detachment of MPs confronted the black soldiers and many shots were fired by both parties. Although several bullets found their intended targets, mercifully there was only one fatality.

It must be remembered that this was wartime and blackout regulations were in place. There were no street lamps, and the only illuminations that night were from the muzzles of rifles, carbines, and pistols as they discharged their lethal contents. It was one of these random missiles that struck William Crossland in the back as he stood defiantly with his comrades at the corner of Co-operative Street and Station Road. His scream of mortal pain appeared to bring both sides to their senses. The shooting became less intense as one of his comrades, who had been standing by him, shouted loudly as he cradled his head in his lap, 'He's dead – Billy's dead – oh Lord, how did it come to this?'

As the shooting ceased, the MPs and the black soldiers gathered up their injured comrades and made their way back to their respective camps. William Crossland's limp body was carried almost ceremoniously back to Adams Hall camp with the entourage of his distraught comrades weeping unashamedly. So how had it come to this? The battle had been fought in a dreamlike state, but this poor limp body had awoken them all to what had been not a dream – but a bloody nightmare.

As it happened, Private William Crossland was not dead, but he was mortally wounded. He was rushed to hospital but sadly, two days later he succumbed to his wounds and died.

Although the battle had come to an inglorious conclusion, the black soldiers were savvy enough to realise that this would not be the end of the matter – and they were right!

Chapter 21

The Aftermath

As the sun rose higher on the morning of the 25th, the streets of Bamber Bridge were eerily quiet. Station Road should have been bustling with people going to their work at the various cotton mills in the town, but they had been told to stay at home that morning. There was however much feverish activity on the roads where the pitched battles had been fought just a few hours earlier. It was the 'clean up' team and consisted of MPs in fatigues and a consignment of policemen from the local constabulary.

Their task was to clear the street of spent cartridges, the occasional discarded rifle, broken glass from the many shattered windows and the splintered remains of the level crossing gates. Following close behind was a fire engine from the local station faced with the unsavoury task of swilling away the many pools of congealed blood that stained the roads and pavements; the largest deposit being on the corner of Co-operative Street and Station

Road, where Private Crossland had met his inglorious and untimely end.

The grisly task having been completed saw a return to near normality, as residents were allowed to go about their daily business once again. The mood however among the town's residents was sombre as the truth emerged as to what had happened in their usually quiet town. This solemn mood was to last for several days.

It was no surprise when later that morning a convoy consisting of army personnel and both military and civil police vehicles pulled into Adams Hall camp. After a brief conversation with the acting camp commander, Major Heris, an order was issued for all black soldiers to assemble on the camp's parade ground.

'I have here a list of all the soldiers who were absent without leave from the camp last night,' he announced grimly. 'As I call out the names, I want those men to step forward.' Minutes later a line of about 35 very fearful black soldiers stood before the Major. With a heavy heart, he turned to the soldiers, MPs, and assembled policemen.

'Gentlemen! Do your duty,' was his order.

Handcuffs were snapped on the wrists of the now terrified soldiers, as they were bundled into the waiting security vehicles, to be transported away for further interrogation.

One of the soldiers involved in this detention exercise that day was Bombardier William Leslie White of the Royal Artillery. His son David relates that at the time his father was billeted locally with a Mrs Livesey in Brownedge Road. It was a duty that had to be carried out, but as he told his son later, one that he didn't particularly enjoy being part of.

The lot of the arrested black soldiers was not a happy

one; they were kept in close detention until a military trial could be held. It was to be two months later before the first of the two trials occurred.

It is hard to believe, but the charity baseball match mentioned in an earlier chapter, actually took place just two days after the battle on June 26th, when a crowd of 7,000 attended a Wings for Victory charity game at Deepdale, the home of Preston North End football club. The Washington Hall Yankees of the Eighth Air Force Control Depot, lost to the Adams Hall Double Clutchers of the Quartermaster Truck Regiment, 13-3.

Adams Hall Camp Guardhouse

Chapter 22

The First Trial - Riot

As it transpired, there were to be two trials. The reason for this was because the first incident was judged by the military authorities to be a riot, while the second, more serious incident, was classified as mutiny.

The first trial was held at Washington Hall, an American Army base in Chorley, just a few miles from Bamber Bridge. It was concerned with the original brawl that occurred when the black GIs were on their way back to camp, after the earlier altercation at the Hob Inn.

The main instigators were identified as Privates Eugene Nunn, Lynn Adams, William Ogletree, and James Wise. William Crossland would also have been on that charge list, but unfortunately, he was now answering to a higher authority. And so, on the 17th of August 1943, the first trial began.

The trial lasted for two days, and despite appeals from the defence lawyers for leniency, all four were found guilty.

The Sentences were as follows.

Privates Ogletree, Nunn and Adams: dishonourable discharge, with total forfeitures and confinement with hard labour for three years. Private Wise: dishonourable discharge, total forfeitures, and confinement with hard labour for two years and six months. The confinement to be in the United States at the Disciplinary Barracks, Fort Leavenworth, Kansas.

Some of the soldiers who were on trial

Chapter 23

The Second Trial - Mutiny

The second trial took place at Eighth Army Air Force Headquarters at Bushy Park, Teddington. This far lengthier hearing was held in two parts. The first lasted from September 3rd to the 9th, and the second part from September 11th to the 19th. One of the men convicted at the first trial, along with the man who was acquitted, were among the 35 accused of mutiny, seizing arms, rioting, firing upon officers and MPs, ignoring orders, and failing to disperse when ordered to do so.

Although the trial was lengthy and went into great detail, especially with regards to the wounded officers and MPs, nowhere is there any mention in the court transcript of the one fatality that occurred, that of the cowardly shooting in the back of black soldier, Private William Crossland. Is there a reason for this omission? Would the mention of it have weakened the case for the prosecution? We'll probably never know the answer to that one. Suffice it to say that

Private Crossland was buried with full military honours, at the American military cemetery, in Cambridgeshire.

At the conclusion of the trial, seven soldiers were found not guilty, seven soldiers received sentences of 12 years or more, and the remaining soldiers received prison sentences varying from three months to 15 months.

However, the President of the Court Martial made an immediate plea for clemency, arguing that there had been an appalling lack of discipline at the camp, and poor leadership, with officers failing to perform their duties properly, and strong evidence physical racial incidents and slurs from many of the MPs. These are his exact words.

'It is quite apparent that their acts resulted in great part from lack of able leadership on the part of their superiors. The evidence clearly established an appalling state of discipline and training in the unit and at the station where they were serving. Many of the officers, whose job it was to guide and control the action of their men, utterly failed in the performance of these duties, and refused to meet and accept responsibility. Had these officers exercised the degree of proficiency normally expected, it is reasonable to assume that the offenses might never have been committed, or at least would not have reached such serious proportions. Although it is recognized that these facts do not excuse the misconduct of the accused, they nevertheless serve to explain the underlying cause of the disorder, and to lessen the degree of guilt of the accused.'

His views were accepted by higher authority, and all sentences were reduced. A year later 15 of the men were restored to duty, and six others had their sentences reduced to one year. The longest period served was 13 months. Opinions on the fairness of the trial varied. Some thought it a kangaroo court, with the defence team being inadequately prepared and performing poorly. Others believed that the board had bent over backwards to be fair. It could be argued that the sentences were very light, considering that they had been charged with mutiny in the time of war.

General Ira C. Eaker, commander of the Eighth Air Force, placed the majority of the blame on the white officers and MPs, and to prevent such an incident happening again, he combined the black trucking units into a single special command. The ranks of this command were purged of inexperienced and racist officers, and along with the MP patrols were racially integrated. Morale among black troops stationed in England improved, and the rates of courts-martial fell. Although there were several more minor conflicts between black and white American troops in Britain during the remainder of the war, there were no further incidents as serious as the one that took place in Bamber Bridge, on that infamous night in June 1943.

Lilian Jones gets her marching orders

AMERICAN RED CROSS

Adams Hall,
Aero Club,
Mounsey Rd,
Bamber Bridge,
Lancs.

4/10/45.

TO WHOM IT MAY CONCERN.

Mrs. L. Johns of ~~---------~~, Bamber Bridge
has been employed from 28/8/44 to 3/10/45 as
Cafeteria Hand at the above Aero Club Canteen.

She has carried out her duties to our entire
satisfaction and we have found her to be
honest, conscientious and reliable.   We
confidently recommend her for any post which
she may seek.

Celia Holmes
Manageress.

"To furnish volunteer aid to the sick and wounded of armies ....." and "To act in matters of voluntary relief
with the military and naval authorities as a medium of communication between the people of the United ....
and their Army and Navy ....."   The Charter of The American National Red Cross.   By Act of Congress

Chapter 23

The Final days

Despite the horrors of what happened in Bamber Bridge in June 1943, an even greater horror, the second world war, was still raging on many fronts throughout the world.

The military duties carried out at Adams Hall camp continued non-stop and would do so until the end of the war – with one major difference.

After the pronouncement by General Ira C. Eaker, a number of selected white GIs were introduced into the trucking unit at the Adams Hall camp. The number of black officers and NCOs was increased, and the new camp commander ensured that there would be no racial segregation anywhere within the confines of the camp. These newly introduced changes ensured that for the remainder of the war in Europe and the far East, there was complete harmony in the camp, and there were no further disturbances either in the camp or the town.

This harmony was further ensured by a similar purging

of personnel with racist views in the ranks of the US Military Police. The introduction of black MPs also proved to be a significant factor in maintaining peaceful relations between black troops and the military law enforcers.

After the Japanese surrender in August 1945, Adams Hall camp began the long process of closing down. By late December of that year, the camp was all but deserted. The majority of the troops, both black and white, had returned to their homes in the USA, after first saying their goodbyes to the many friends they had made in the little northern mill town of Bamber Bridge. Despite the troubles of June 1943, the townspeople had taken to the African

Sergeant Peter Delia
One of the last GIs
at the Camp

American GIs, and there was great sadness in the town when the camp gates closed for the last time. Their stay in the UK had proved to be a watershed for them. They had seen first-hand that black and white people could live in harmony, and it is from these early revelations that the seeds of racial integration were sown.

After the end of the war, Jim Crow continued to exert his racist influence in the US, particularly in the Southern

The Red Cross ladies and a couple of GIs in the final days

States, but his days were numbered. Bamber Bridge and its residents can be duly proud of the part they played in their contribution to the eventual introduction of US laws, that would give their black citizens the same civil rights as the rest of the nation.

The last of Adams Hall Camp prior to demolition to make way for a much-needed housing estate

Old Hob Inn where the memorial will be located
Copyright GEOFF WILKINSON (cc-by-sa2.0)

Epilogue

As memories fade, it is important for the sake of future generations, that the Battle of Bamber Bridge is remembered. Not for the violence that occurred that night in June, but for the underlying reasons as to why fellow Americans fought against each other.

Racism and bigotry were undoubtedly the reasons, and to ensure such incidents can never happen again, and that each passing generation is aware of what can happen when racism and bigotry are rife, a memorial to this effect is to be erected in the town of Bamber Bridge. It will be built in a community garden near the Hob Inn where the first incident that sparked the battle took place.

9 781838 276928